Four Letters Spell Love: H-E-L-P

JASE SERIES
BOOK FOUR

Written by Jason Crabb
Illustrated by Anita DuFalla

Printed in the United States of America   ISBN 978-0-9888994-3-8   www.jasoncrabb.com

The JASE Series is dedicated to my girls: my beautiful wife, Shellye,
and our precious daughters, Ashleigh and Emma. You mean the world to me.
With love from our family to yours:
Jason, **A**shleigh, **S**hellye, and **E**mma.

Special thanks to Philip and Tina Morris and Donna Scuderi for your creative input and love of the cause.

Number
4

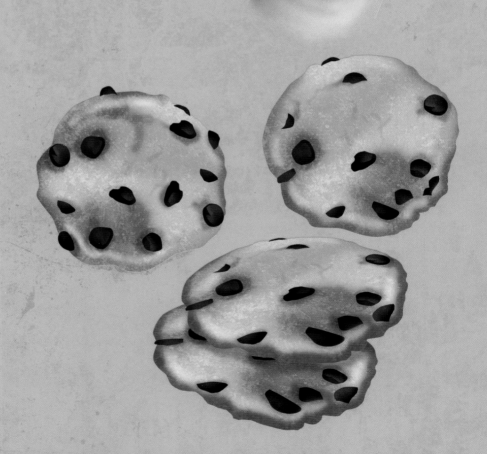

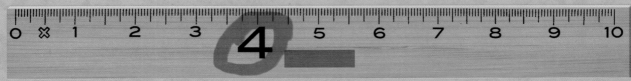

The 4th Commandment

For Crabb Kids

God's day of rest is for you — and for your crab, too.

1. **Love God more than all, even crabs great and small.**

2. **Friend and crab, while you love them, always see God above them.**

3. **Don't be crabby toward God. Say His name with your love.**

4. **God's day of rest is for you — and for your crab, too.**

5. **All children and crabs, respect Mom and Dad.**

6. **Don't hurt one another, not a crab or your brother.**

7. **Crab or person alike: love your husband or wife.**

8. **Never steal from your brother, your crab, or another.**

9. **Little boys, girls, and crabs, tell the truth and be glad.**

10. **Be sure to enjoy your stuff and your crab, not wishing for something your neighbor has.**

Jase was with his friend, Mateo,
when he saw a girl at another table.
Her bouncing pigtails caught his eye.
Her smile was sweet, but she seemed shy.

Jase walked over, and once he was there,
he noticed her special chair.

"My name's Jase. What is yours?"
She giggled when she saw his claw.

"I didn't mean to laugh," she said.

"Oh," he replied, "I'm always red!"

"My name's Lily. You make me smile.
Would you come and stay with us awhile?"

"Sure!" Jase said. "I've got my stuff."

"Well, Mister Crabb, follow us!"

Jase asked her dad,
"May, I come?"
He said, "You're very
welcome, son."

"For my short legs, this ramp is cool!"

She answered, "It's no fun at school."

"The kids," she said, "they all know
that I can't manage on my own.
They watch the lift and always stare
at me and at my special chair."

Jase thought a moment and said, "It's true.
Your chair is special and so are you!
We all need help, and every day
God sends His help in special ways."

"Help comes from chairs,
and dads, and friends.
Our loving God made
all of them!"

"Let's go," said Jase, "where we can look at love in God's amazing Book.

It shows exactly what love means when someone has a special need."

13

"See this crowd? They're here because **Jesus** came to **share His love.**"

14

"He's inside, helping folks.
There's no room left, we can't get close."

15

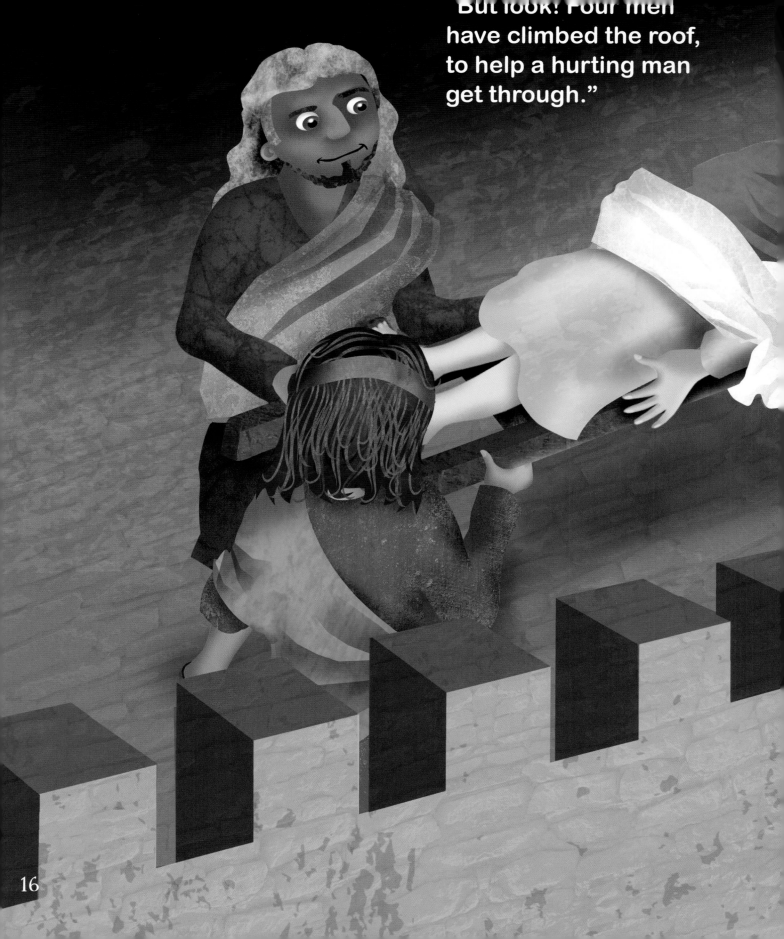

"Wow, Jase! They carried him up high.
Without their help, he couldn't try."
(Mark 2:2-4)

"With help," said Jase, "he'll meet Jesus,
the One who loves to bless and free us."

"It's time to go. It's almost night…"

"But now," said Lily "I see the light!"

"When others help and show their love,
they're listening to God above.
When we are helped, He is pleased.
The love He sends us meets our needs!"

"Yes, young lady! Now off to sleep.
Tomorrow is church for you and me.
God's day of rest is good for you,
your family, and your crab friend, too!"

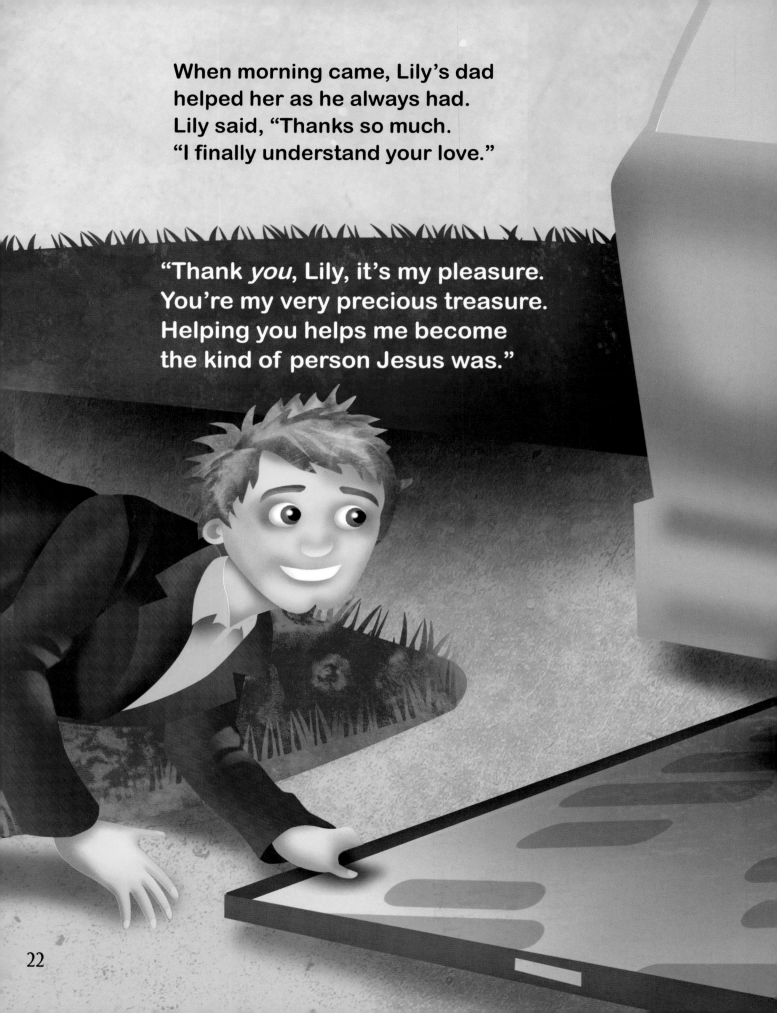

When morning came, Lily's dad
helped her as he always had.
Lily said, "Thanks so much.
"I finally understand your love."

"Thank *you*, Lily, it's my pleasure.
You're my very precious treasure.
Helping you helps me become
the kind of person Jesus was."

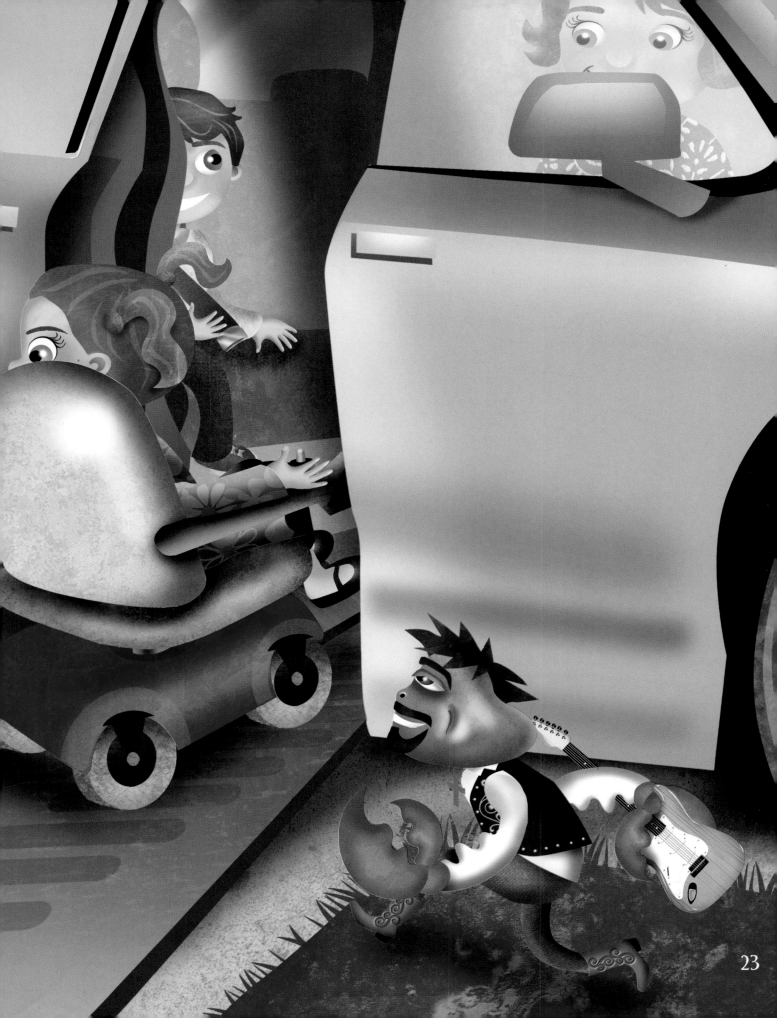

Joyfully they sang their way to church as one big family

When they arrived, Lily's friends
Ashleigh and Emma said,
"Let us help! Let's go inside."
Lily answered, "Thank you, guys!"

25

When they were done, they waved good-bye. But something else caught Jase's eye.

"Lily, do you know who those boys are? There…those two!"

"Yes, I see them every week. One is funny. One rarely speaks."

Jase knew what Lily said was right about the boys who dressed alike.

He knew that God was sending him to share His love with the twins.

Jase smiled real big
and told them, "Hi."

What happens next is in Book Five!

Jase® — A "Crabb" With a Mission

Children are precious — to us and to God! And their growing-up years are so important to the people they become. Through their everyday experiences, children discover their individual identities, their unique destinies, and the reality of their loving Creator.

When faced with challenges and disappointments, children are comforted to learn that other children share many of the same experiences. As they hear other children's stories, they are strengthened in discovering that they are not alone, or "more strange," or "less courageous" than their peers.

The vision for The Jase® Series took root in my heart two decades ago. Now, as a husband and the father of two beautiful girls, I long to reach children and those who love and care for them with the Good News—the gospel of Jesus Christ! I pray that this children's story will sing the melody of God's heart to yours, whatever your age.

— Jason Crabb

coming up next in the Jase series

In a continuing dreamland adventure, Jase® and his twin friends, Lucas and Liam, witness David's victory over Goliath—and Lucas, who is vision impaired, gains a new self-image.

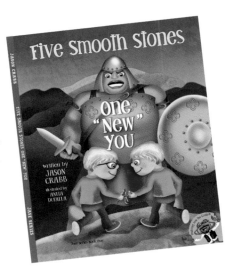

Hey kids!

Now that you've read the book, how would you like to:

- Download Jase FUN pages
- Access the Jase and You Review
- Earn a diploma from Jase University
- And more ...

Go with me to **www.jasecrabb.com** to continue our journey together!!!